One day Jelly and Bean went to play hide and seek among the trees.

Jelly ran to hide while Bean counted up to ten.

"One ... two ... three ... four ... five ...," said Bean.

Jelly ran to a wide oak tree.

She saw a crack in the trunk.

" … six … seven … eight …," said Bean.

Jelly went to hide inside the crack in the wide tree trunk.

" … nine … ten," said Bean.

"I am coming."

Bean went to look for Jelly. She was keeping still inside the wide tree trunk.

"Buzz ... buzz ... zzz." Oh no! There were bees inside the wide tree trunk. There was a beehive in it. "Buzz ... zzz ... buzz."

Jelly jumped out of the wide tree trunk. "Help! Help! There are bees inside this tree trunk," she said. She made a dive for the bushes.

Bean saw Jelly.

Then he saw the bees.

Bean made a dive for the bushes too.

The bees buzzed over the bushes for a little while.
Then they went back to the beehive in the wide tree trunk.

"I do NOT like bees," said Jelly.

"It must be time for a sleep."

So the cats went back to the little shed and fell asleep.

"i-e"

hide

while

five

wide

nine

inside

beehive

dive

like

time

High Frequency Words

day and went to play the up
cats said a in I am look for
was no of are this like it she
they he

one trees ran two three saw
there were out help made then
too over back do not must be
so little jumped